WOMEN'S RIGHTS IN NIGERIA

ADEOLA BABATUNDE

For more information about this publication, send your mail to info@love2work.org

Printed in Great Britain

CONTENTS

INTRODUCTION

The name Nigeria was suggested by British journalist Flora Shaw in the 1890s. She referred to the area as Nigeria, after the Niger River, which dominates much of the country's landscape. The word niger is Latin for black.

More than 250 ethnic tribes call present-day Nigeria home. The three largest and most dominant ethnic groups are the Hausa, Yoruba, and Igbo (pronounced ee-bo). Other smaller groups include the Fulani, Ijaw, Kanuri, Ibibio, Tiv, and Edo. Prior to their conquest by Europeans, these ethnic groups had separate and independent histories. Their grouping together into a single entity known as Nigeria was a construct of their British colonisers.

In general, labour is divided in Nigerian society along gender lines. Very few women are active in the political and professional arenas. In urban areas, increasing numbers of women are becoming involved in the professional workforce, but they are greatly outnumbered by their male counterparts. Women who do manage to gain professional employment rarely make it into the higher levels of management.

However, women in Nigeria still play significant roles in the economy, especially in rural areas. Women are often expected to earn significant portions of the family income. As a rule, men have little obligation to provide for their wives or children. Therefore women have traditionally had to farm or sell homemade products in the local market to ensure that they could feed and clothe their children. The division of labour along gender lines even exists within industries. For example, the kinds of crops that women cultivate differ from those that men cultivate. In Igbo society, yams are seen as men's crops, while beans and cassava are seen as women's crops. Modern Nigeria is a patriarchal society. Men are dominant over women in virtually all areas. While Nigeria is a signatory to the international Convention on Equality for Women, it means little to the average Nigerian woman. Women still have fewer legal rights than men. According to Nigeria's Penal Code, men have the right to beat their wives as long as they do not cause permanent physical injury. Wives are often seen as little more than possessions and are subject to the rule of their husbands.

The struggle for women's rights has gained momentum during the past two decades. Beginning with the 1975 International Women's Year (IWY) World conference and the IWY Tribune in Mexico City, continuing through the Women's World Conferences and the series of agenda-setting UN World conferences on Women in Beijing. Women have developed and discovered new skills and tools that they are now using to leverage for change on behalf of women's rights at global, country and community levels.

Unfortunately, a large proportion of women themselves are ignorant of many of their rights and the laws which protect them.
Yet, the knowledge of these Instruments is perhaps the most powerful tool. Society has already stereotyped gender roles, which hinder the recognition and enforcement of women's rights.

The issue of gender inequality has of recent come to the fore in the struggle for women's empowerment and emancipation in Nigeria. Nigeria is a mainly patrilineal society where gender relations are based on the patriarchal point of view.

The traditional role of a woman is that of a child bearer, home keeper, comforter and cook for her husband, children and larger family. This pre-supposes the propagations of the male as the superior sex for purposes of inheritance, marriage and family relations, political participation and power relations including family and social decision-making.

Traditional practices regarding widows and the female child lend weight to the marginalisation of women. Domestic violence is accepted as a way of calling erring women to other. Societal values and perceptions, which regards women as inferior to men are the critical factors in shaping behaviours to women.

In effect, women cannot actualise their rights without the active support and participation of other stakeholders in the society such as the police, magistrates, Judges, Lawyers, the community leaders, the traditional rulers and medical Doctors who can play various roles in the promotion and enforcement of women's rights. These roles sometimes complement each other.

This book is directed at women. It addresses the deficiencies in the capacity of the stakeholders mentioned above. It also addresses factors which could be implemented to improve the effectiveness of women's rights and thus close the gap between the theory and actual implementation of human rights that women should enjoy.

Chapter one is about women's human rights in secular and religious legal system. It also talks about the rights guaranteed by International Instrument and the Nigerian constitution since the constitution is the basic law of the land from which all other legislation derive their legacies.

Chapter two talks about the issue of gender inequality as it affects the role of women in contemporary Nigerian Society.

chapter three talks about the reasons why it is so difficult to stop discrimination against women in Nigeria

Chapter four suggests the various things that could be done to help stop the infringement upon the rights of women in Nigeria.

CHAPTER ONE
Women's Rights in Secular/ Religious Sphere

CHAPTER ONE

Women's Rights in Secular/ Religious Sphere

Human rights are increasingly becoming the main concern of the World community as a whole. Chapter IV, section 30 -40 of the Nigerian constitution dealt with the rights of her citizens. The sections states that all Nigerian citizens automatically have the right to good food, Shelter, standard living and rights to participate in decisions or activities which affects or relates to them in the community. These rights complement what is stated under Article 2 of the Universal declaration of Human Rights (1948). The article states that the right shall be for all, regardless of their sex.

United Nations also provided a supplementary documents which are meant to be followed when talking about rights of women.
They are:-
.Marriage should be a voluntary thing and a minimum age should be applicable.
.A stop to be put to trafficking in women and slavery should be abolished.
.Social and political rights for women should be addressed .
.Determination of the nationality of married women

1.1 CONCEPTIONALISATION OF TERMS

"Women's Human Rights"

Although the "Convention on the Elimination Of All Forms of Discrimination Against Women" (CEDAW) was ratified without reservation in 1985, Nigerian women are still discriminated against

Women's Rights in Secular/ Religious Sphere

and have to struggle for the recognition of their basic rights. This is because the protections offered to women under CEDAW are non-justiciable under the 1999 constitution of the federal Republic of Nigeria. Furthermore, Women's rights guaranteed under law are undermined by poverty, lack of access to education and established social practices which accord women a subordinate role to men and constrain women's opportunity to participate in the public arena. Thus, women are discriminated against in all sectors of society-employment, the political process, education, property ownership and inheritance rights, among others.

The coexistence of three overlapping legal systems (the common law and statutory law, Muslim laws and customary law) make it difficult to enforce laws which protect women's rights. Again, the constitutional provision on fundamental Rights make no distinction between the rights of Men and women. This is a serious omission considering the extent of discrimination against women both in law and in practice. For example, women are disadvantaged by the law on assault and sexual assault:

.Federal law does not regard wife battery as a crime if it:
"does not amount to the infliction of grievous bodily harm… done by the husband for the purpose of correcting his " and if the offence is subject to any native or customary law in which such correction is recognised as law"
.The Criminal Code Act (Law of the Federation) {221} makes it impossible to secure conviction for the sexual assault or defilement

Women's Rights in Secular/ Religious Sphere

of girls under 16 on the   "uncorroborated evidence of   one witness";

.The Criminal Code {353} makes indecent assault on men a felony punishable with up to three years   imprisonment; section 360 makes same crime against   women a misdemeanour and punishable by up to two years;

.Divorce on the ground of domestic violence is only Permitted where the respondent has been convicted to attempted murder or of intentionally inflicting harm within one year of date of filing for divorce. {16{1}e   matrimonial causes Act}.

The Law on rape is weak:

.Marital rape is not recognised as a crime; a man who "inflicts extensive bodily harm on his wife while forcibly
 having sex with her is punished not for sexual offence, but for an ordinary assault";

. Rape victims are not accorded anonymity during trial
 proceedings, which   together with the social stigma attached to rape, may widely discourage women from reporting crimes. *The issues of women's inheritance rights is also a major concern.*

. In traditional, social and religious practice, women's rights to inherit property are unequal to the rights of men. In some cultures, women are regarded as property to be inherited after their husband's death.

Women's Rights in Secular/ Religious Sphere

Although there is no doubt that the apartheid of gender is considerably more pervasive than the apartheid of race, it has never provoked the same degree of International concern or opprobrium. The International community usually couches discussion of the advancement of women in terms of the acquisition and implementation of rights particular to women. While this is certainly an important and valuable project, it can also obscure some basic elements contributing to the oppression of women.

The central argument is that the current International human rights law create obstacles to the advancement of women. Because the law-making institutions of the international legal order have always been and continue to be dominated by men, International human rights law has developed to reflect the experiences of men and largely to exclude those of women, rendering suspect to claim of the objectivity and universality of international human rights law. Until the gendered nature of the human rights system itself is recognised and transformed, no real progress for women can be achieved not only in Nigeria but also in the International societies.

There are problems in speaking about women and their experiences in a global context. Obviously, differences of class, wealth, race and nationality will lead to differing power relationships among women. Some feminists of colour and women from developing nations such as Nigeria have questioned attempts to universalise a particular understanding of feminism, charging white western feminists with inappropriately assuming that their particular concerns are shared worldwide.

Women's Rights in Secular/ Religious Sphere

But patriarchy and the devaluing of women, although manifested differently within different societies, are almost Universal. As peggy Antrobus, Director of the women and Development programme at the University of the West Indies, told the 1991 World Women's congress for a healthy planet:

"Although we are different by race, class, culture and geography, our hope lies in our communities. All women's unremunerated household work is exploited, we all have conflicts in our multiple roles, our sexuality is exploited by men, media and the economy, we struggle for survival and dignity, and rich and poor, we are vulnerable to violence. We share our otherness, our exclusion from decision making at all levels".

1.2 UNIVERSAL DECLARATION ON HUMAN RIGHTS

The universal Declaration of Human Rights (UDHR) is the primary international articulation of the fundamental and inalienable rights of the human family.

It was adopted on December 10,1948 and it represents the first comprehensive agreement among nations as to the specific rights and freedoms of all human beings. It defines human rights broadly and symbolises a World vision of respect for the humanity of all people. While not much is said about women. Article 2 does not entitle all to the rights and freedoms set forth in the Declaration without distinction of any kind, including sex.

Furthermore, when read from the perspective of women's lives, many violations of women's rights such as rape and battering can

Women's Rights in Secular/ Religious Sphere

readily be interpreted as forbidden under existing clauses such as "No one shall be subject to torture or to cruel, inhuman or degrading treatment or punishment"

The problem is that little elaboration of these rights has been made from the point of view of women and therefore, we have no significant body of International human rights law and practice in this area.

International Human rights stated that the term 'human' includes both sex (men and women) as such, whatever provision is made for one sex should automatically apply to the other sex. In practice, the laid down principles of the international human rights is not been followed. For women are seen as an inferior sex to men. There is no point advocating for new laws to be made to spell out the rights of women. In as much as women are also human being and the international human rights stated that the word 'human' applies to both sex, that automatically gives women the same rights as men. What will be needed will be to educate those who are either not informed or not well informed about the meaning of the term 'human' about its true meaning.

1.3 According to the Vienna Declaration:
"The fundamental rights and freedoms are neither obtained, nor granted through any human actions. They may not be recognised or respected in these actions, but they still belong to each individual.

Women's Rights in Secular/ Religious Sphere

The rights, which derive from inherent dignity, are also inalienable. Nobody can deprive anybody of these rights and nobody can renounce these rights by herself or himself. Legal norms (or human rights Law) do not establish fundamental rights and freedoms but only guarantee them"

1.4 Convention on the Elimination of All Forms Of Discrimination Against Women (CEDAW)

Discrimination against women is defined by Article 1 of the United Nations convention on the Elimination of all forms of Discrimination Against women of 1979 (referred to as the 1979 convention of CEDAW) as "any distinction, exclusion or restriction made on the basis of sex which has the effect or purpose of impairing or nullifying the recognition, enjoyment or exercise by women, irrespective of their marital status, on a basis of equality of men and women, of human rights and fundamental freedoms in the political, economic, social, cultural, civil or any field. Nigeria happens to be among the nations that joined the convention on 23 April 1984 and they ratified it without any reservations on June 13 1985. As thus, Nigeria is bound by the laid down rules of the convention and will be expected to follow it without any reservation.

1.5 NIGERIA CONSTITUTION AND HUMAN RIGHTS

The Nigerian constitution is the supreme law of the country and is superior to all other laws. If any law is not consistent with the provisions of the Nigerian constitution then the law is void to the

Women's Rights in Secular/ Religious Sphere

extent of that inconsistency. Therefore, the provisions of the Nigerian constitution, which protect women should be held supreme to all other laws and customary practices.

The Nigerian constitution guarantees certain basic rights to every citizen irrespective of their sex. These rights are called fundamental human rights. Thus, women have the same political, social and civil rights as men do. These rights are also similar to those guaranteed by the Universal Declaration on Human Rights, The African charter on Human and people's rights and Article 2-6 of the CEDAW

Article 46 of the 1999 constitution of Nigeria enables any person who considers that her constitutional rights in chapter IV of the constitution (Fundamental Rights) have been contravened in any state in relation to her to bring a claim in the High Court of the state for redress.

Article 43 makes provision that every citizen shall have the right to acquire and own property anywhere in Nigeria. Article 42(1) states :

"A citizen of Nigeria of a particular community, ethnic group, place of origin, sex, religion or political opinion shall not by reason only that he is such a person:-

(a) be subjected either expressly by, or in the practical application of, any law in force in Nigeria or any executive or administrative action of the government to disabilities or restrictions to which citizens of Nigeria or other communities,

Women's Rights in Secular/ Religious Sphere

ethnic groups, places of origin, sex, religion or political opinions are made subject or;

(b) be accorded either expressly by, or in the practical application of, any law in force in Nigeria or any such executive or administrative action, any privilege or advantage that is not accorded to citizens of Nigeria of other communities, ethnic groups, places or origin, sex, religion or political opinions"

It is therefore possible to plead in any claim brought in the High Court that the application of any law, customary or otherwise, which excludes women from acquiring (Whether by inheritance or succession) or owing (lack of access to loans, capacity provisions etc) property amounts to a disability and restriction and affords a privilege or advantage to men which breaches both article 42 and 43 of the constitution.

Additionally, other provisions of the constitution can be pleaded as part of any claim. Article 15(2) prohibits discrimination on the grounds of sex, inter alia, article 17 (2)(a) states that every citizen shall have equality of rights, obligations and opportunities before the law, article 19 (d) states that the Government's foreign policy objectives shall be respect for International law and treaty obligations and article 21(a) provides that the state shall protect, preserve and promote the Nigerian cultures which enhance human dignity and are consistent with the fundamental objectives as provided in chapter II.

Women's Rights in Secular/ Religious Sphere

These fundamental objectives are principles of non-discrimination, equality under the law and respect for International law including human rights. These objectives enable us to plead International human rights principles as part of the claim to activate the state's positive duty. These include principles in , but not limited to, the constitutive Act of the African Union (article 4(1) promoting gender equality), the non-discriminatory provisions of the convention on the Elimination of All Forms of Discrimination Against women (CEDAW), the African Charter on Human and people's Rights and the protocol to the African Charter on Human Rights on the Rights of women.

IS Human Right Absolute for Women ?

Fortunately, ever since the 1993 World conference on Human Rights in Vienna " Women's rights are human rights" become a rallying cry for women all around the World. Thus, since women are humans, what applies to humans applies to women. Hence, all the rights guaranteed by the Nigerian constitution to "every person" applies to women.

1.6 WHAT ARE THE RIGHTS PROTECTED?

Chapter 4 , sections 33-34 of the Nigerian constitution (1999) made provisions for the rights to life, right to personal liberty, right to freedom, right to freedom of expression, right to freedom from discrimination and the right to acquire properties of all her citizens.

Also, chapter 2, section 15 of the constitution states that discrimination on the grounds of sex shall be prohibited. While

Women's Rights in Secular/ Religious Sphere

section 17 upholds that 'The social order is founded on the ideals of freedom, equality and Justice. The sanctity of human person shall be recognised and enhanced."

Right to Life
No one can take a woman's life except by a judgment of court. Therefore, it is an abuse of a woman's right to be killed by her husband or male partner. There are many cases of male violence (wife beating, acid bath or assault) within family relationship, which has resulted in the death of the women (femicide) and the men responsible are not brought to justice.

Human Dignity
The Nigerian constitution guarantees the right to dignity of the human person; consequently, no person should be tortured, put to inhuman or degrading position, or forced into labour or held in slavery or servitude. Women being humans are entitles to the right to Dignity equally as men.

Similar protection of the dignity of women is contained in the African Charter, Convention on the Elimination of all Forms of Discrimination Against women (CEDAW), Declaration on the Elimination of all forms of violence against women (1993) and the Universal Declaration on Human Rights(UDHR) Even though the constitution categorically identified the rights of women, it is not been followed. Such stipulations could be seen in theory as 'Tiger paper' in practice, women are still seen as inferior to men.

Women's Rights in Secular/ Religious Sphere

Their roles in the community has not changed from the usual child bearing, looking after their children and their husband and taking care of the home chores.

Women are considered to be people who can be seen but not heard. In Northern Nigeria, women are not even seen! They are considered tools and properties of men 'whose superior position had been obtained by the divine powers or the society'. Culturally, almost every evil doctrine in society is attributed to women who are often humiliated and accused of being responsible for the deaths of their husbands and children.

In practice, Nigerian women suffer inhuman treatment and loss of dignity in many ways such as female circumcision or genital mutilation, dehumanizing widow- hood Practices, servitude, trafficking in women under exploitative and slave-like conditions, which are violations of human dignity. Some of the perpetrators of these degrading treatment are women as for example the enforcement of de-humanising widowhood practices are women (e.g. "the Umuada" in the Ibo Culture)

The recent introduction of the sharia Islamic law by some states in the Northern part of Nigeria which permits sentencing of women to stoning for adultery, or awards corporal punishment of canning degrades the dignity of women and is contrary to the rights guaranteed by the Nigerian constitution. In many parts of Nigeria, Discrimination in girls' access to education persists owing to

Women's Rights in Secular/ Religious Sphere

customary attitudes such as, early marriage and pregnancies, inadequate and gender biased teaching and educational materials, sexual harassment and lack of adequate and physically and otherwise accessible schooling facilities. The United Nations Chronicles acknowledged that there is gross inequality between men and women in the area of rights in the Country.

Freedom and security of person

Women cannot be detained without trial or imprisoned without good reason. Torture is not allowed. Violence, cruel punishment or inhuman treatment is not allowed. This provision should stop men abusing their wives or even parents abusing their Children. Slavery, servitude and forced labour are not allowed.

Personal Liberty

Some women are prevented by their husbands from going out to work. No woman can be deprived of her personal liberty. A woman may not be arrested and held without good reason(s). If charged with a crime, one has the right to be presumed innocent until proven guilty.

Right to privacy

A woman cannot be searched or have her home or possessions searched without legal authority. Her correspondence, telephone conversations and telegrams are protected. (Sec 37 constitution, Art 12 UDHR, Art 17 political Rights covenant)

Women's Rights in Secular/ Religious Sphere

Freedom of Religion, Belief and opinion

Every woman can believe or think whatever she wants. Follow any religion she chooses. State Institutions (like school) can follow religious practices but they cannot force her to participate in a particular religious practice. (Sec 38 constitution; Art 18 UDHR)

Freedom of Expression and Press

Women have the right to freely express themselves, that is say what they want and the press can say what they want too. But they may be prevented by law from spreading hate or encouraging people to violence. This is the law, unfortunately by customs and traditions, a woman is to be seen not heard. Indeed, a woman who is very vocal in public is viewed with degree of odium. *(Sec 39 constitution, Art 19 UDHR, Art 20 ICCPR, CEDAW)*

Peaceful Assembly and Association

There is the right to gather peacefully and associate with others in public or private. No one can force anyone to join any group if she does not wish to do so. A Citizen can only join a registered political party if he/she wants to participate in partisan politics, however, it is common knowledge that husbands forbid their wives to take part in partisan politics and make life difficult for them if they insist on doing so. In many cases, this leads to the marriage being broken.

Freedom Of Movement

Everyone can go to or move about anywhere freely throughout Nigeria and to live anywhere they want in the Country. One can even

Women's Rights in Secular/ Religious Sphere

leave Nigeria if one wishes and come back at any time if one is a citizen. However, the immigration insists that a married woman cannot obtain a passport without the written consent of the husband. Many women trade across borders and they must have valid travelling documents. Thus, the action of insisting on the husband's written consent for a passport is a violation of the constitution and surely the fundamental rights of women.

(Art 13 UDHR Art 12 ICCPR & CEDAW)

Freedom from Discrimination

The constitution provides as a fundamental right equality of all persons irrespective of sex, ethnic affiliation, place of origin and religious or political opinion. This right to equality is very central to the promotion of other rights of women. International and Regional Instruments such as CEDAW, UDHR,ICCPR, and African Charter also guarantee this right to equality. Consequently, women are guaranteed freedom from discrimination on account of their sex.

Right to property

The constitution gives right for citizens to possess properties and such property can only be taken by the government if the law dealing with this applies to everyone or if it is going to be used for a public purpose or in the public interest and if so, such person is entitled to adequate compensation. **(Sec. 43, 44)**

Women's Rights in Secular/ Religious Sphere

Right to Education

The constitution guarantees the right to education, regardless of whether male or female. This constitutional guarantee is re-iterated in the convention for the rights of the child which has been ratified by Nigeria. A female child should not be denied education merely because she is female. Parents should not deny the girl children from acquiring education merely because they will get married and move to their husband's house. It is a violation of the rights of the girls-child which will hamper the development of such children.

Language and Culture

Everyone can use the language and follow the culture that they choose but they must respect other people's human rights when they do so.

Political Participation and Governance

Women have the right to take part in the Government of the Country. Women can vote and be voted for so long as they are adults and not disqualified according to law.

An adult is anyone above the age of 18 years. **(Art. 21 UDHR, CEDAW 7 & 8)**

CHAPTER TWO
Gender inequality in Africa

CHAPTER 2

Gender inequality in Africa

Gender generally refers to the differences in the social functions and power relations of men and women (and to a large extent child). Gender is to do with the differences in the roles of women and men, the differences in what is expected of them by society and how both should be treated by virtue of existing differences.

Gender mainstreaming therefore implies a deliberate and proactive effort to bear in mind the implications of any decision, plan, implementation or project on both men and women. Gender mainstreaming therefore means that all plans, decisions and management are guided by gender considerations.

In Africa, society has been generally patriarchal. This implies that power; resources, decision making and control have been dominated by men. This is not to suggest that women did not or do not have any roles to play at all in Africa. Women have their roles but these roles are also controlled by men. Such is the status of women in Africa. Even after independence, the situation did not change much. Nonetheless Africa has witnessed the wave of women emancipation campaigns that have been on going in recent years. The International Conferences on Women in Nairobi and Beijing opened an environment of intense advocacy for women's emancipation and gender equality. Serious activism has since developed across Africa and there have also been proactive efforts to improve the situation of women in Africa. The Charter of the Organisation of African Unity (OAU) 1963 did not generally provide for gender equality and the protection of women.

Gender inequality in Africa

Its main concern was the preservation of African independence and combating colonialism and interference in the domestic affairs of sovereign African States. In relation to gender and women, it was sadly inadequate.

The African Union (AU) Constitutive Act 2001 provides expressly that one of the principles of the AU is gender balance and equality. The AU has since gone ahead to establish a Declaration on Gender Equality in Africa whereby at least 50 % of all the members of the Commission of the AU had to be women. Indeed many African governments have attempted to appoint many women to political positions of decision making and influence. In several African countries many women are parliamentarians and cabinet ministers. Such is the situation in countries like South Africa, Rwanda, Uganda and Kenya.

The question is now whether the above developments have brought concrete improvements in gender equality and balance in Africa. It is also a massive question as to whether they have improved the situation of women Vis a Vis conflict and the role that women can play in preserving peace and ending conflict. The answer in the opinion of this Paper is no! This Paper contends that efforts at gender equality and balance must be complemented by concrete respect, promotion and protection of human rights. The situation of women's rights Vis a Vis conflict in Africa is now analysed.

Gender inequality in Africa

(i) Women's Rights and Conflict in Africa

Women's rights in Africa generally can be looked at within the framework of the African Regional Human Rights System. The African Regional Human Rights System is basically based on the African Charter on Human and Peoples' Rights (ACHPR) (1981). The African Charter was adopted by the former OAU Assembly of Heads of State and Government (AHSG) (now referred to as the AU Assembly) in Nairobi Kenya in June 1981.

The Charter is a unique instrument of human rights in several senses. It was the first international human rights instrument that provided for all categories of human rights (Civil political, socio economic and group rights) in a single document.

The Charter creates the African Commission on Human Rights. But the Charter is also discredited with what are called claw back clauses. These are provisions that appear to take away given rights. These so called claw back clauses create limits on several given rights. In relation to women, the Charter is terribly weak. The Charter only expresses provides for the protection of women's rights in a single article that also provides for the protection of children and the family. It has been argued that the Charter indeed puts women and children on the same footing and in a subservient role in a family. The Charter provides nothing for the involvement of women in conflict transformation. The Charter equally provides nothing express for the involvement of women in decision making or representation, apart from a general provision on equality and prohibition of unfair

Gender inequality in Africa

discrimination. The Charter is also without provisions on other areas that are crucial to women in situations of conflict. Such are Violence against Women, rape and war crimes.

It has hence been recognised that there is need to have a specific instrument that caters for the rights if women in Africa. It has been hoped that such an instrument would galvanise all efforts and activities that aim at gender equality and protection of women's rights in Africa.

(ii)The Protocol on Women's Rights in Africa

The Protocol to the African Charter on Human and Peoples' on the Rights of Women in Africa 2003 (the Protocol on Women or the African Women Protocol), is an attempt to effect the identification, promotion, fulfilment and protection of women's rights in Africa in both the private and public spheres. It is specifically structured to take care of the situation of women in Africa, against a background of socio-economic and cultural obstacles.

The Protocol was adopted by the Assembly of the AU on 11 July 2003 in Maputo Mozambique. This was after a protracted process of debate among the selected representatives of AU states. It was realised after the coming into force of the African Charter, that women's rights remained inadequately protected in terms of the available framework in Africa. The situation of women definitely remained highly vulnerable to human rights abuse even after the coming into force of the African Charter. Sexual and gender

Gender inequality in Africa

imbalance remained. As a result of this gender bias, a number of activists and organisations clamoured for the transformation of the African human rights discourse to more closely reflect women's experiences.

The Protocol is a fairly big departure from the African Charter in relation to the protection of women's rights in Africa. Some of its provisions on the protection of women are analysed in turn, with an emphasis on women and conflict:

The rights to Life, Integrity, and Security of the Woman
The Protocol provides for the protection of women's right to life and human security.

While the Protocol provides for the protection of the women's right to life and their security in article 4, it does not consider several relevant matters. For instance it omits to touch upon rape as a weapon of war in a comprehensive way. Yet, in recent times rape has been used as a weapon of war and genocide against women. It also follows that many of the women that were raped for instance in the 1994 Rwanda Genocide contracted HIV. The Protocol should have usefully covered such an aspect.

(iii)Gender Issue under the Nigerian Context
The issue of gender inequality has of recent come to the fore in the struggle for woman's empowerment and emancipation in Nigeria. Nigeria is mainly a patrilineal society As such, it is believed that the

Gender inequality in Africa

traditional role of a woman is that of a child-bearer, home keeper, comforter and food provider.

Traditional practices regarding widows and the female child lend weight to the marginalisation of women. Domestic violence is accepted as a way of calling erring women together. Social values which regards women as inferior to men are the critical factors in shaping behaviours to women.

Over the years and with civilisation, not much has changed. The capitalist, economic system acquired during colonisation equally adversely affected the status of women because women were disadvantaged in entering the changing economic market due to the dominant role of men in public affairs. The Victorian societal view of the woman as the home keeper reduced the influence of women and therefore their role in public affairs. This added to the traditional palmachial system further reduced the status of women in public decision making. It is common sense that those who make policies and make decisions will do what is more beneficial to them.

Should women strive to assert their equality to, or difference from, men? Hence, might equality be achieved through claims for equal rights with men or should the law be encourages to acknowledge difference? Given that we live in a society constructed by men and in which men currently hold privileged positions, which option represents the most attractive proposition for women? Before being able to respond to these questions it is necessary to ascertain what "equality" means. In this respect it is appropriate to make a

Gender inequality in Africa

distinction between equal treatment, equal opportunities and equal consequences. Failure to provide maternity provision in the workplace means that men and women are treated equally. But because women usually undertake the role of primary carer for their children , it may be that employment opportunities available to men and women differ as a result and that women suffer discrimination. People frequently claim that they are entitled to equality: to equal opportunities, equal treatment, equal protection of the law, or perhaps even an equal distribution of material goods. These sorts of claims to equality are much like claims to Justice.

Equal treatment and just treatment may be the same thing. We know that equality and justice are closely connected, but what the connection is has always generated considerable controversy. The old Aristotelian notion of procedural justice enjoins us to treat like cases alike and unlike cases differently in proportion to their differences. According to this formula (which is certainly one of the most widely accepted propositions in the history of philosophy and law), the puzzle of equality has three pieces.

First, are men and women (or Christian and Jews, blacks and whites, rich and poor, or educated and illiterate) relevantly similar or different? This is the question on which most of history is focused. Second, once we have identified who is alike or equal, what does it mean to treat these equals alike? What is equal opportunity, equal treatment, or equal protection of the law? Third, if people can be different but still equal , what does it mean to treat different cases in

Gender inequality in Africa

proportion to their differences? This last question has hardly been discussed at all in traditional legal and philosophical discourse, but it is central to recent feminist discussions of equality.

It is this presumption (the presumption of inequality) that began to change in the seventeenth century, with movements for the recognition of universal or human rights and democratic, constitutional government.

Women have always been , and still are , denied equal rights on the ground that they are different and therefore not equal. One can say that all men are created equal, but we do not act as though it were true. Furthermore, we did not even say that women are equal to men until very recently and even now the claim is very controversial.

For example, because women are considered different from men, they could be banned from universities, libraries, businesses and professions. It was simply up to the legislatures (which of course were composed entirely of men) to deal with such matters as they saw fit. If they felt that it was indecent or 'unladylike' for any woman to practice law, carpentry, bartending , or medicine, they could deny all women a licence to practice, simply on the ground that they are women. Such action in the United States would violate the constitutional rights of men, but because women are considered different, they had no constitutional rights to equal protection of the law. It did no good to appeal to the courts. In theory, Women are noted to have the same right as men under the Constitution of the

Gender inequality in Africa

Federal Republic of Nigeria yet, in practice, women are treated under the law differently from Men. One can say that Women have all the rights written in the constitution but that which they do not have is that which will equate them to men.

2.1 Areas Of Inequality

. *Labour and employment*

Women do not generally earn the same wages as men for the same work. Especially, casual or organised labour which is where most women are employed. Those in public service are discriminated against in the area of maternity, sexual harassment and employment practices.

. *Access to finances and credit*

Most banks and finance homes do not give loans to women and most times, women have to be guaranteed by men before they can access credit for economic activities. This results in more women becoming poorer, even those who are able to do some business for their economic enhancement.

. *Politics and Participation*

Women are not equipped to participate effectively in Politics because of low esteem and inability to jump the hurdles set by the men. Such hurdles include rigging, money politics, thugery, membership of "boys clubs" there exists only gender tokenism for women in politics. Women do not have the financial resources to compete in the high financial game of politics in Nigeria. They are therefore given positions which the men do not find lucrative or challenging enough.

Gender inequality in Africa

Thus, politically, women's rights are denied because of poor representation at the levels where decisions and policies are made.

- ### Education and Health Care
Inadequate education and inadequate facilities for health care hinders women's quest for equality, unhealthy and uneducated women cannot produce healthy children or engage effectively in social activities.

- ### Harmful Traditional Practices
Traditional practices like female genital mutilation, widowhood practices, male preference, domestic violence lend weight to discrimination in women. The heavy work load of women within the household and lack of house decision making powers is another way by which women have been deprived of their right. Male preference leads to abuse and low esteem for the female child even from birth and thus she does not develop her full potentials to enable her contribute effectively to the nation.

- ### Violence Against Women
Women are still victims of rape, sexual assault, sexual harassment, assault and battery, widowhood practices, forced labour, trafficking, incest, and other forms of gender assaults and abuses. Domestic violence is still regarded as a private affair requiring no legal or official intervention.

- ### Access to Justice
Women are politically, economically, socially, culturally, educationally and legally disadvantaged. They cannot take advantage of facilities and opportunities available to them to achieve

Gender inequality in Africa

and enforce their human rights. They are mostly ignorant of their fundamental rights and freedoms. In many Police stations, women are still not allowed to take people on bail.

Women's International network (WIN) acknowledges the long-standing nature and ubiquity of women's economic power in Nigerian society. Concluding "(Women have always had some economic power and have exerted influence in Nigerian society through Women's council, family connections and to a much lesser extent, mainstream social, economic or political organisations"

The report recognises that in Nigeria there are regional religious and ethnical variations in the pattern of discrimination against women, but indicates that men are legally able to prevent their wives from working, from obtaining passports, and rural men routinely beat their wives without any legal intervention. Access to land and right to inheritance of spousal property are also denied women, as is access to Jobs for single women. Given the record of Government non-performance, it is also questionable whether Nigerian women's rights organisations would believe in the veracity of its promise to investigate.

The protection and expansion of women's rights then is clearly another instance where the exercise of power by affluent countries is taken for granted, and the readiness of poor countries to submit themselves to scrutiny while never examining the affluent country's behaviour is also taken as a marker of responsible International behaviour. Nigerian "government publicly opposes female

Gender inequality in Africa

circumcision, which reportedly affects close to 50 percent of the female population, the most dangerous form, infibulations, is still practiced in some areas. However, because of the deep cultural roots of this practice, the government has relied primarily on education through women's and public health organisations to help induce change in attitudes rather than trying to criminalise the practice. Public education has had some effect, but change has been slow. The government also opposes the selling of young girls for marriage by poor rural families, again primarily through educational means. There are no estimates of the extent to which this practice is carried out.

In the Northern part of the country (Nigeria) , Girls are not given the opportunity to go to school. Education was seen to be meant only for boys. Few of the girls who by chance were able to have the slight chance of education have it cut short by early marriage and childbearing. These in essence made it difficult for women to be seen as been productive in the community. Instead of women been seen in big production companies as the men, what women end up doing because of their little level of education is a small farm and selling petty commodities.

It will be right to say that Gender and class are important factors limiting women's achievements in Nigeria. Jobs such as Doctors, Lawyers Engineering and architecture are for men because of their educational qualifications.

"The discriminatory burdens placed on women include those of chastity, of making marriage work at all cost, of fertility and fertility

Gender inequality in Africa

control, and the burden of being "clean and desirable" as symbolised by female circumcision. Others include the burden to prove rape both in the community and in a court of law, to raise 'good' children, and to morn their husband to the taste and dictate of his relatives. Compared to men, Nigerian society treats women as little better than beasts of burden ..."

This illustrates a bias that automatically assumes that traditional societies were bastion of reactionary and unprogressive practices that marginalised women. Temisanren refines the argument about pre-colonial sources of discrimination against women, contending that some practices may have been relevant at the time they emerged but have become questionable given the changes in society over time. Temisanren documents Yoruba women's attempts at guaranteeing abortion rights but claims that these women are manipulated, thus undermining their autonomy.

Another source of problems that militate against women's rights in Nigeria is that most of the administrative practices which prevent equal treatment of Nigerian Men and women are products of Colonial Laws and government. A case in point is the legal assumption that only males are the heads of families. Another is the assumption that a woman must prove that she was not responsible for bringing discriminatory practices upon herself. A third problem arises from the lack of resources to pursue the legal remedies that may be available. While there are admirable and significant efforts being made by

Gender inequality in Africa

some lawyers and women's groups to provide free legal assistance, these efforts remain inadequate.

2.2 Discrimination against women under the religious (sharia) and Customary Laws and practices

Examining the constitution indirectly itself there are areas of discrimination against women. First, the language of the constitution indirectly discriminates against women by use of the masculine term to describe both female and male.

The section on Citizenship gives only Men right to acquire citizenship for their foreign wives and no reciprocal right for women to pass on their Citizenship to their foreign husbands. This negates the provision of the constitution for equality as women have the right to be treated as Men. Contrary to the constitutional guarantee of freedom from discrimination, women suffer discrimination under the guise of customs and religious practices. For example, at birth the female child is not as welcomed as the male child because of the traditional preference for male children, resulting from the patrilineal system.

The discrimination continues throughout the life circle of the woman from childhood where she faces overwork in home, then at adolescent subjected to forced or early marriage. She is married out at early age. Sometimes the married child bears children which may be injurious to her health making her have the health problem of vesico vagina Fitula (VVF), a condition which subjects a child to the lack of control of the victims urinary and excreting organs. As a result

Gender inequality in Africa

of which the young drains uncontrollably of faeces and urine causing further health problems.

In the home, the girl is over burden with work doing household chores while her male counterpart is allowed to play. At marriage, the woman faces physical and sexual assault in form of wife beating or domestic violence, rape including marital rape.

In the unfortunate death of the husband she suffers obnoxious widowhood practices. Some of which involves the shaving of the widow's hair, the denial of basic hygienic practices for periods as sign of mourning, and in some places the forcible drinking of the water used to bath the corpse of the disease as proof of her innocence in the death of the husband.

At old age. Especially, if the woman is childless, she is branded a witch and may be stoned to death. At each stage, the woman goes through experiences that diminish her humanity starting from rejection for being female to genital mutilation to lack of equal opportunity to education, heavy workload in the household and unequal treatment with male siblings.

2.3 Women's Rights Under Sharia Law In Nigeria

In the religious participation, women are relegated to the background and are not permitted to take leadership roles. Contrary to the express provision of the Holy Quran which does not state that women should not go to the place of worship when doing their

Gender inequality in Africa

menstruation, women are forbidden from going to the mosque when menstruating. The Holy Quran in fact stated as follows;

"O you who believe, when the congregational prayer (Salat Al Jumu `ah) is announced on Friday, you shall hasten to the commemoration of God, and drop all business. This is better for you, if you only knew" The Holy Quran did not say only men should go to the place of worship to Almighty Allah.

"Women have been victims of discrimination since sharia was extended to criminal law in northern Nigeria, both in terms of certain provisions in the new sharia legislation and the other practices and regulations enforced outside the framework of the law" While some of these practices existed prior to the introduction of the legislation in 2000, and have been considered a part of daily social life in northern Nigeria for many years.

The political climate since 2000 has encouraged discriminatory behaviour towards women by providing a new, official framework for it, and human rights violations against women have increased. As stated by a Nigerian academic and activist in Kaduna (Northern part of Nigeria), "although it is difficult separating the Hausa and Islam patriarchal structure, the reintroduction or politicisation of sharia in northern Nigeria has contributed in reinforcing traditional, religious and cultural prejudice against women"

Discrimination against women is institutionalised in parts of the sharia criminal legislation in force in northern Nigeria. There are two main provisions in the law which discriminate against women. The first in the inequality in the weight of testimony. According to the

Gender inequality in Africa

Sharia penal codes, a woman's testimony as evidence in a trial is worth half that of a man, or the testimony of one male witness equals that of two female witnesses.

The second aspect which discriminates against women is the inequality in standards of evidence in cases of Zina (extra-marital sex, which is referred to as adultery if the person is married, or fornication, if she is not). Women have been adversely affected in these cases. Under the sharia codes in force in Nigeria, based on the Maliki school of thought, pregnancy is considered sufficient evidence to convict a woman of adultery. For the male defendant, on the other hand, the sharia penal code requires that the act of adultery must have been witnessed by four independent individuals before the man can be convicted – a standard of proof which is usually impossible to obtain, and has not been obtained in any of the cases which have arisen so far. This glaring discrimination in standards of evidence has had serious consequences for women charged with Zina. It has resulted in situations such as those of Bariya Magazu, Safiya Husseini and Amina Lawal, where the women were found guilty and sentenced to death, or flogging, on the basis of their pregnancy, whereas the Men named in the cases were acquitted for lack of evidence.

There have also been cases when men have been convicted for adultery, but these convictions have usually been based on the Man's own confession. Even provisions of Sharia within the Maliki school have been applied selectively. For example, Judges have

Gender inequality in Africa

considered a woman's pregnancy as sufficient evidence of Zina, yet have ignored the provision of the "Sleeping embryo", which exists within the same school of thought and is more favourable to female defendants. In the case of both Amina Lawal and Safiya Husseini, the option of accepting that the baby could have been fathered by the woman's husband was disregarded by the Judges who initially sentenced the Women. In the case of Amina Lawal, however, the Katsina state Sharia Court of Appeal accepted the argument of the "Sleeping embryo" as one of the grounds for concluding that Amina's baby could have been conceived with her husband.

The plight of women before the Sharia courts, especially in cases of adultery, has been aggravated by the absence of women in the Judiciary. There are no female judges in the sharia courts, as the Maliki school of thought prohibits women from becoming Judges.

The vast majority of the defence lawyers are also Men. One of the few female lawyers to have acted on behalf of women sentenced by sharia courts was initially prevented from speaking in court by the Sharia court Judge, on the basis that female defence lawyers could only speak through the male counsels on their teams.

Judges have also failed to investigate allegations of rape made by female defendants in adultery cases and have ended up punishing some women who claimed to have been victims of rape. For example, in the case of Bariya Magazu, the teenage girl accused of extra-marital sex who accused three men of raping her, the Judge not only failed to order an investigation into her claims but charged

Gender inequality in Africa

her with falsely accusing the three men, who had denied having sexual relations with her.

In the Sharia penal codes, rape is a crime punishable by death, if the offender is married, or by flogging, if the offender is unmarried. However, the inequality in the standards of evidence required for men and for women means that, in practice, it is more likely that a woman who alleges she has been raped will be found guilty of adultery, or possibly false accusation, than the man charged with rape.

In addition to the discrimination they face in criminal cases before sharia courts, women have faced other forms of discrimination in their day-to-day life, affecting, among other things, their freedom of movement and freedom of association. Since the advent of sharia, some state government have introduced measures to prevent men and women from being seen together publicly.

These measures, most of which are not codified into laws, have been applied most stringently in Zamfara state, where the state government prohibited Men and women from travelling together in public transport, such as buses, taxis and motorbikes commonly used as taxis, known as *Kabu –kabu.*

Especially in the period immediately after sharia was introduced, the hisbah frequently stopped taxis which carried male and female passengers together and made the women disembark. There were

Gender inequality in Africa

cases during this early period, where *kabu-kabu* drivers were charged and flogged for carrying female passengers. The government introduced and provided separate vehicles for men and women. On larger buses, men and women were made to sit separately, with men at the front and women at the back. This was one of several requirements codified in a law passed in zamfara state on May 31, 2001, and violations of this requirement were punished by "reprimand, exhortation or warning; or fine not exceeding N500:00 or both.

The restrictions on travel by *kabu-kabu* which is the most common and sometimes the only form of transport in many areas – was especially harsh on women, some of whom had to walk long distances because the drivers (who are always male) refused to carry them or simply drove past them. Car drivers who assisted women in this situation by offering them a lift were also sometimes stopped and harassed by the hisbah. In 2001, Christians formed their own taxi drivers' association, partly in protest at these restrictions and partly in a bid to make up for lost earnings. Christian drivers carry a special identity card indicating that they are members of the Association of Christian Motorcycle Operations and accept female passengers.

Women were also under increasing pressure to dress in a way which conformed to the notion of what was considered appropriate according to Islam. However, in most states, the dress code was not clearly defined, and was interpreted differently by different individuals,

Gender inequality in Africa

even among the religious and political establishment. As with other issues, such as "immoral gatherings", there was considerable confusion arising from attempts by the hisbah to enforce some kind of dress code in the absence of a legally prescribed code. There are several cases in Kano state when hisbah had stopped women in connection with their style of dress.

Most Muslim women in Northern Nigeria traditionally covered their heads, even before Sharia was extended in 2000, so many of them have not experienced a significant difference in this respect. However, some said that their mode of dress was supervised more closely by the hisbah since the extension of sharia, and that the issue was now more publicised. In Kaduna State, the hisbah organised lectures for women on how to dress, but did not approach them individually if they judged that they failed to comply. In kano, the hisbah sometimes stopped women who were not 'properly dressed' took them to their office, gave them a lecture, then gave them a hijab (veil). In some areas, public pressure on women to cover themselves completely intensified. For example, sometime around July 2003 there were graffiti on walls: "Watch your mode of dress- sharia" and "Dress properly, or else. Sharia"

Most of the attempts to enforce a dress code for women have been undertaken by the hisbah, rather than the state governments.

The exception is Zamfara state, where a law was passed in 2001 prohibiting "Indecent dressing in public" as well "Indecent hair cuts" for both men and women. Regarding women, the law specifies:

Gender inequality in Africa

"Every female of Islamic faith shall put on dress to cover her entire body except for her feet, hand and face in the public or while attending the office both within or outside the state.

One of the most serious cases where women were directly victimised for not conforming to a particular dress code occurred in Bauchi State. In February 2002, twenty-two Christian nurses were suspended from their jobs at the Federal Medical Centre in Azare for refusing to wear a uniform based on Islamic dress, which the hospital director had introduced to replace the standard nurses' uniforms; the hospital stopped paying their salaries. Eventually, ten of them agreed to conform to the dress code simply in order to be able to resume work. However, the remaining eleven did not, and were fired on April 24, 2002.

It is a ground for divorce under Sharia for a man to assault his wife even though a man has the right to admonish his wife. The instrument used must be symbolic with a toothbrush or chewing stick and must not leave a mark on her body. Beating will be an example of injury and discord between husband and wife. She will need to prove assault by calling a witness. In a divorce granted under the condition, the woman does not need to return the gift (or mahr) given to her in the course of the marriage.

Sharia law allows the man to withdraw maintenance from the wife if she denies him sex but the law generally forbids marital rape.

Gender inequality in Africa

Consequences of Marriage under Sharia Law as it affects women's rights

.The husband has a right of correction and chastisement of the wife.

.The husband has a right to demand full obedience to all his orders and instructions provided it does not conflict with the wife's obedience to Allah.

. The wife cannot go out without the permission of the husband.

Customary Law Challenges:

(a) Inheritance and property rights

Under Yoruba customary law, the immoveable property of the head or founder of the family, usually the Father/husband, becomes family property for the use and possession of his descendants, both immediate and future, on his death or intestacy. Daughters have the same rights as sons over their father's property. They are entitled to remain in the family house, which becomes family property to which all have rights of possession equally. These rights do not terminate on marriage and in the case of divorce, they may return to the family house with their own children.

As in the case of **coker .v. coker** . As wives, women do not inherit from their husbands nor do men inherit from their wives. The customary law position has been further supported in case law which

Gender inequality in Africa

confirmed that Yoruba native law and custom deprived the wife of inheritance rights in her deceased's husband's estate because devolution of property followed blood.

As members of the family, daughters and sisters, women enjoy in theory full rights in the use and enjoyment or the proceeds thereof of family property. In **Thomasia Ayoola Ricardo .v. John Lajorin Abal,** it was held that a woman's sex does not deprive her of her fundamental rights as a senior member of the family in relation to junior members in age of the family. On partition men and women take in equal proportions.

However, on marriage, their rights are de facto curtailed because they are considered full members of their husband's family and are expected to participate and concentrate their efforts on their new family.

Obligations that are a corollary to the rights of the family property membership such as participation in family meetings and councils, consultations on family matters may not be capable of being fulfilled and, in practice, this may be regarded as curtailing the rights.

Fundamentally, the most important right of family property membership is possession and by residing elsewhere, most women, on marriage, unless they have returned on divorce or separation, will not be able to fulfil the most fundamental right.

By the custom of some areas, the woman herself is property and can be inherited. The payment of bride price equates the woman to a

Gender inequality in Africa

purchased item to be inherited. For example, despite the advancement of the Yoruba culture which permits the female child to inherit on equal basis the position of the female as a wife is quite discriminatory as she is not permitted to inherit from her deceased husband's estate.

In the case of **Akinubi .v. Akinubi**, Mrs Rufus was married under the Yoruba customary Law and blessed with 5 children. Her husband died without writing a will. The deceased owned a storey building, which was let to Owena Bank. The deceased brother applied for and obtained letters of administration which the wife opposed and sought an injunction to restrain them from functioning as administrators of her husband's estate. The trial court ruled that the wife had no locus to institute the action, she being under customary law herself a part of her husband's estate. She appealed but the court of Appeal dismissed her appeal. On further appeal to the supreme court, it was held:

"it is a well settled rule of native law and custom of the Yoruba that a wife could not inherit her husband's property. Indeed, under the Yoruba customary Law, a widow under an intestacy is regarded as a part of the estate of her deceased husband to be administered or inherited by the deceased's family, she could neither be entitled to apply for a grant of letters of administration nor appointed as co0administrix"

The decision of the above case is against the right of women to the fundamental human right of equality guaranteed by the constitution,

Gender inequality in Africa

CEDAW, UDHR African Charter and other International Instruments signed by Nigeria. It shows the cultural bias that women are not to be treated equally.

Widows have no rights and such rights that they do have are dependent on the right of their children, if any, to residency in the family property. The rationale for this lack of rights may be attributed to the whole notion of family property. All women will have some rights in the family property of their natal home.
However, having not exercised that right during the duration of their marriage, they may be stopped not in law (since they are entitled to return to the property by law) but in practice, from exercising that right after the death of their husbands because they will not have been able to perform the obligations of family property membership. Consequently, upon marriage, women's rights with regard to family property falls into the interstices between law and practice.

Generally, women married under statutory law are entitled by law to inherit parts of both their deceased husband's real and personal property. Daughters are entitled to share equally with their brothers the real and personal estate of their father. There is no discrimination in law as to who may apply for letters of administration ; the wife is entitled to do so jointly with any of the children who have attained majority. The core problem in these cases, however, is that custom is predominantly enforced. This may be due to ignorance of rights under the law or pressure by kin to follow tradition. If death rites are

Gender inequality in Africa

performed according to custom, pressure to deal with property after burial according to tradition may not be easily avoided.

Enforcement of rights using the legal system is not common; financial constraints may be a factor and perhaps also an unwillingness to go through the legal process. Where there is no legal support for discrimination, cultural practices militate against women's rights.

Under the Customary law, a man has the right to correct his wife if necessary by beating. By Igbo custom, a man chastise his wife for failing to perform her duties, laziness, wastefulness and destruction.

(b) Customary law: Child custody

As a result of the patriachial system, there is a general belief that Children belong to the father. This notion has been outlawed by the provision of the customary courts Laws of the various states constituting the old western region. This provision provides that:

"In any matter relating to the guardianship and custody of children, the interest of and welfare of the child shall be the first and paramount consideration"

In practice, the customary courts headed mostly by men usually award custody of children to the men particularly the male children. So also are decisions made by Traditional Rulers in adjudicating over such matters in their domain do not follow the law laid down in customary courts laws. However, there are now cases where the courts have decided issues of custody based on the welfare and

Gender inequality in Africa

interest of the children being of paramount consideration. i.e, **Okwueze vs. Okwueze** A highly contested custody which started in the Ondo customary court and ended in the supreme court. There were 5 issues of the marriage all under the age of 16, custody of the children had been awarded by the customary court to their father, irrespective of the fact that the customary court laws applicable in Ondo state provided that, "in any issue relating to the custody or guardianship of children, the welfare of the children shall be the paramount consideration"

About seven years later when the appeal finally arrived at the supreme court, it was held that the welfare of the children was a question of fact to be determined by a consideration of many factors means that the court had not done justice to the case, consequently, the supreme court order a retrial of the custody issue in order to ascertain where the best interest of the children lay.

(c)   Customary Law and Women's rights in employment

Married women are discriminated against in employment and under the tax policies, many employers are reluctant to employ married women because of reluctance of the employers to grant some rights and privileges arising from their marital or pregnancy status.

Some women are denied employment for being of childbearing age. The responsibility of childbearing or reproduction is not considered as service to the society by most employers. Consequently, employers consider it a loss to accommodate the time when the women went to perform their reproductive responsibilities. Women are also usually denied maternity leave in private countries.

Gender inequality in Africa

Although the Tax laws have been made gender neutral after much agitations from women's groups for equal treatment, the application of the tax laws in Nigeria still discriminate against women. This is because women have to prove "beyond reasonable doubt" that they are the breadwinners in the homes before being allowed the tax relieves. Whereas a man need not prove that he is married or that he has children or that he maintains his children before he benefits from the tax relief. Some women are denied employment for being of childbearing age.

Family and tradition: While some women have made considerable individual progress, both in the academic and business world, women remain underprivileged.

Although women are not barred legally from owning land, under some customary land tenure systems only men can own land, and women can gain access to land only through marriage or family.

In addition many customary practices do not recognize a women's right to inherit her husband's property, and many widows are rendered destitute when their in-laws take virtually all of the deceased husband's property.

Widows are subjected to unfavourable conditions as a result of discriminatory traditional customs and economic deprivation. "Confinement" is the most common rite of deprivation to which widows are subjected, and it occurs predominately in eastern Nigeria.

Gender inequality in Africa

Confined widows are under restrictions for as long as 1 year and usually are required to shave their heads and dress in black garments. In other areas, a widow is considered a part of her husband's property, to be "inherited" by his family. Polygyny continues to be practiced widely among all ethnic groups and among Christians as well as Muslims and practitioners of traditional persuasions. Women are required by law to obtain permission from a male family member to get a passport. The testimony of women is not equal to that of men in Shari' a court.

The Government only occasionally criticized child abuse and neglect, and it made little effort to stop customary practices harmful to children, such as the sale of young girls into marriage.

There were credible reports that poor families sell their daughters into marriage as a means of supplementing their income. Young girls often are forced into marriage as soon as they reach puberty, regardless of age, in order to prevent the "indecency" associated with premarital sex. Female Genital Mutilation is practiced among all ethnic and religious groups. According to an NNC study, an estimated 33 per cent of all households practice the procedure.

CHAPTER THREE

Women in Contemporary African Context

CHAPTER 3

Women in contemporary African context

The role assigned to men and women is pre-determined by societal attitudes. Women's role is seen as reproductive and not productive. Hence, the false dichotomy between private and public spheres and the values placed on marriage and motherhood.

Moreover, CEDAW etc has its limitations. The standard of equal protection – that the state shall not treat gender violence with any less seriousness than other forms of violence – often fails in the absence of crime statistics in the private sphere and it may be argued that human rights laws ought to deal directly with the substance of gender-specific abuse, and not just the failures to provide equal protection to women. However, in the absence of "National homicide data by gender" for most countries of which Nigeria is included, it is difficult to show " systematic non-prosecution" pattern, often a necessary threshold to establish responsibility. Given that " the institution of the family is also an arena where historical power relations are often played out" the state would be called upon to adopt special corrective measures rather than the usual levels of supervision. There are also some problems under the evaluation of Rights Discourse under the gender treaty language. **They are:-**

.   **Rights and the imbalance of power**

At the core of the rights issue, in both national and International law, is the fact that legal rights do not stand alone; they are embedded in the dominant social and cultural milieu. As a result, the interpretation of rights guaranteed by an International treaty occurs at the inter-

Women in contemporary African context

section of the legal system and the social system. When Judges interpret applicable law in individual cases, the law is "read" in the subjective, social realm. There, the interpretation of the legal "right" becomes subject to the dominant cultural paradigm – an engendered, socially constructed World, where Women's experience is seldom recognised. When the interpretation is undertaken by a man (which it often is) or by a woman who has been socialised to accept the male elite's norms and interests as her own, the law is subjected to the interpretation of a Judge whose approach to the Law constructs women's lives from a male-centred perspective.

The history of Judge's interpretation of Laws affecting women in the United states demonstrates that the "objective" application of law is a socially constructed enterprise. Critical legal theorists drive this point home through evaluation of such cases as ***General Electric company .v. Gilbert***, in which Justice Rehnquist's majority opinion asserted that the exclusion of pregnancy-related disabilities from an employers' health insurance plan did not have a desperate effect on women since pregnancy was an "extra" disability that only women suffered. The exclusion of pregnancy ensured the equality of the plan with respect to men by using men as the measure against which to determine the "equality" of the plans coverage, justice. Rehnquist revealed the inherent male-orientated bias in his reasoning; according to his reasoning, "pregnant persons", while men, along with non-pregnant women, were simply "non-pregnant persons"

Women in contemporary African context

• Rights and political Action

Many of the provisions in the Women's convention that use gender-neutral language play this symbolic role, which is an essential first step to beginning the difficult work of changing the distribution of burdens and benefits in a society.

Nevertheless, a strategy based solely on the acquisition of equal legal rights using current "male" rights as a standard may provide benefits for women that are more symbolic than actual. In some contexts, moreover, this strategies may have pitfalls. Although legal rights do not necessarily translate into actual equality of opportunities within a given society, the successful acquisition of rights may lead to decreased activism within a social movement if activists come to believe that the battle has been won.

The recognition that equal rights often fail to reflect the realities of women's lives (and are often hampered by the very legal system designed to enforce them) thus highlights the shortcomings of Universal treaties phrased predominantly in gender-neutral language. The failure to respond to women's voices, combined with the inherent bias of those empowered to interpret, apply and enforce law has the potential to severely undermine the efficacy of laws written in gender-neutral language.

.Un equal Employment Opportunities

Equal employment opportunity and associated rights are provided for in Article 11 of the CEDAW. The Nigerian constitution of 1979 also

Women in contemporary African context

provides that the government endeavours to ensure "equal pay for equal work without discrimination on account of sex or on any ground whatsoever". Unfortunately, it is not the case in Nigeria, for men still largely control the commanding heights of both politics and the economy.

It is clear that the primary responsibility for domestic labour falls on women despite the provision that parents "share the same rights and responsibilities" by Article 16, 1, d, of the 1979 covenant. Until men and women bear equal responsibility for household labour, women will have limited access to employment opportunities and upward mobility.

.Enforcement /Implementation Challenges

Case law demonstrates that judges do not always question the validity of customary laws or indeed the gender aspects of customary laws in the light of the constitutional protection, regional treaty obligations and international treaty obligations. In a 1994 case, ***Olowu .v. Olowu*** Bini customary law on inheritance was confirmed. The eldest or first son of the deceased inherits exclusively the last house where the deceased lived and died and if he had only one house, the first son inherits the house to the exclusion of all the other children.

The case concerned the estate of a Yoruba man who naturalised as a Bini man. One of the deceased's sons contested the devolution of the property under this tradition amongst other issues. Ige J.C.A said on that matter, "If the appellant has any grudge against Bini Native

Women in contemporary African context

Law and Custom he should have objected to his father's naturalisation as a Bini man in the lifetime of the father and not wait to contest ownership of a house which he was looking forward to inherit"

In the case of *Akinnubi .v. Akinnubi*, the deceased's wife was bequeathed to the deceased's younger brother according to tradition. Since the tradition is correct, the court made no comment on the practice or the value judgments behind them. Once the customary law or tradition has been verified, the courts tend not to question the law it elf or at least consider any gender aspects which ought to be incorporated for a modern society.

.Non-compliance with the rules laid down in CEDAW

The convention on the Elimination of all Forms of Discrimination Against Women, (CEDAW) which Nigeria has ratified without reservations requires states parties, under article2(f) and under Article 5, to take appropriate measures to abolish customs and practice which constitute discrimination against women. Discrimination practices also breach article 18(3) of the African Charter on Human and people's Rights which says that "The state shall ensure the elimination of every discrimination against the woman and the child as stipulated in international declarations and conventions"

There are various instances of discrimination against women: Yoruba customary law on custody of the child belonging to the father clearly breaches Nigeria's obligations under CEDAW, since Yoruba

Women in contemporary African context

women do not have equal rights of custody or guardianship. Current practice also breaches article 8 of the protocol to the African Charter on Human and people's rights on the rights of women on equality between sexes, and article 6 on equal rights in marriage.

While Yoruba women already have the right to own and acquire property (article 6 (j), the application of a requirement of possession of the family property operates to exclude them from benefiting from their right to property.

It is a failure of the state that laws are not being applied and implemented. It is a failure of the judiciary that refuses to look behind the operation of customary law practices that discriminate when they have the tools to hand with constitutional, continental and international law practice that can be used. The supremacy of customary law in the area of family law means that the status quo with regards to discriminatory practices remains unlikely to change unless legal rights are enforced by litigation.

CHAPTER FOUR

Issues of Concern

CHAPTER 4

Issues of Concern

In terms of domestic protections, of the problems militating against the elimination of discrimination against women, most important is the fact that de jure guarantees do not necessarily imply de facto recognition. Imam argues that the Nigerian social structure favours men over women, resulting in exploitation which effectively subordinates women in all spheres of life. For this exploitation to be eliminated, structural change must occur. The most desirable form of change must be multi-dimensional in nature, incorporating changes in state legal policy as well as in social policy. In addition, power relations in the family must change. However, it is refreshing that more recent scholarship is subjecting the argument of generalized male dominance in Nigerian society to closer scrutiny.

The consensus emerging is that more study has to be done to highlight examples that contradict generalizations of male dominance in Nigerian society.

Concrete steps to change the social structure must include mass organization among women, directed at surmounting the class divisions among them. This is necessary for purposes of consciousness-raising, as well as for developing a common front to emphasize and promote in political debate. Since most discrimination is justified by references to culture, evidence about the positive role of women in pre-colonial Nigeria should be presented and widely promoted to counter negative stereotypes.

Issues of Concern

Despite Nigeria's gruelling economic crisis, the education of women must be given utmost priority to enhance their ability to exercise self-determination in the control over their bodies and to participate as equals in the labour force. Education must also be extended to the rest of society on the importance of promoting and protecting women's rights. The involvement of more women in policymaking within the government at local, regional and federal levels must be further instituted and entrenched. Some steps have been taken in this direction by the Federal Government of Nigeria which, beginning under the Mohammed/ Obasanjo administration, made the appointment of one woman in every decision making and consultative body mandatory. However, there must also be legal reforms which enhance the protection of the rights of women in Nigeria and remove present abuses by calling for the equal application of administrative procedures.

Constraints limiting the elimination of discrimination against women also arise from the nature of the international system which seeks to formalize these protections. Some of these problems can be attributed to the relative newness of this body of rights and the institutionalized procedures for promoting and protecting them.

The Committee on the Elimination of all forms of Discrimination Against Women is the body vested with the authority to investigate, review and evaluate the performance of states which are parties to the Convention (Articles 17-20, CEDAW). Unfortunately, the Committee lacks adequate resources for enforcing legal guarantees

Issues of Concern

within the CEDAW and receives inadequate cooperation from members, which are in large part slow in submitting reports. Moreover, several countries including the United States have thus far not ratified the CEDAW, or have introduced many reservations which makes CEDAW meaningless. In cases where the CEDAW has been ratified, mechanisms for self-enforcement are unavailable. International protections currently are basically exhortatory in nature and do not carry the force of law. An additional problem arises from the need for the Committee to coordinate and integrate its work with other UN organs dealing with women.

A problem with international guarantees is that signatories to the CEDAW are expected to introduce constitutional and legislative changes, which give effect to its protections. Governments are then expected to make periodic reports on the progress made (Art.2). Such self-policing leaves room for abuses._Due to these and other problems, the Committee has been somewhat limited in its ability to live up to its potential. The same problems apply to regional protections.

There is no doubt that the elimination of discrimination against women involves much more than legal protections and social engineering. It is obvious that activism among women, which has always been an important part of Nigerian life, must continue. In addition, there must be more cooperative action among women of all classes and in all areas of Nigeria. Their guiding principle must be the one found already in some groups in the country--as long as

Issues of Concern

some women still live under discriminatory conditions, all women are affected. There must also be the fine-tuning of national, regional and international protections in order to remove elements of vagueness, combat inaccurate portrayals of women as well as provide more concrete enforcement mechanisms to guarantee more effectively the rights of women. These protections must be seen as building blocks in a constantly evolving process.

The male dominant elements of Nigerian Society remain strong. Many of these elements are located within the family, where a woman is required to take care of her husband and home. Since most women also work outside the home, this creates, a double burden and may limit the ability of women to devote an equal amount of attention and concentration to their careers or trade. In Nigeria law and administrative practice, the predominant attitude is that men are the household heads and have primary authority. This attitude persists in spite of past and contemporary examples of cross-gender cooperation in many households and also despite the existence of many female headed family unit.

Although CEDAW guarantees full equality of men and women in the family. However, prevailing practice in Nigeria is to overlook customary and pre-colonial practices which prevent the achievement of full equality. While the government acknowledges the "need for public enlightenment in the area of marriage and family law," by the time its first report to CEDAW was handed in, very little of substance had been done beyond the institution of a pilot legal project on family Law. Today, there is a women's Bureau, which is attached to

Issues of Concern

the office of the Presidency, and a more aggressive stance is taken about improving women's status in the society. Although the programme is only beginning. The better life for Rural Women programme is directed at correcting some of the deficiencies noted in the first report to CEDAW. Since 1979, more women have formally competed for political office.

Also, the role assigned to men and women is pre-determined by societal attitudes. Women's role is seen as reproductive and not productive. Hence, the false dichotomy between private and public spheres and the values placed on marriage and motherhood.

Despite provisions for human rights in the Nigerian Constitution, there are significant problems for women under the current laws. The punishments under Sharia law for criminal offences, conflict with the constitutional guarantees of human rights. Health problems, such as

HIV/AIDS and maternal mortality further add to the plight of women. Women already bear the brunt of poverty and declining services. A few women have been elected to the legislatures but for the most part their involvement in politics is at the grassroots, as were their Aba sisters of 1929. In the colonial era, women lost some of their political power and continue to struggle for rights and recognition in a male dominant society In terms of domestic protection, of the militating against the elimination of discrimination against women, most important is the fact that de jure guarantees do not necessarily imply de facto recognition. It is apparent base on the stated facts that Nigerian social structure favours Men over women, resulting in

Issues of Concern

exploitation which effectively subordinates women in all spheres of life. For this exploitation to be eliminated, structural change must occur.

Until the gendered nature of the human rights system itself is recognised and transformed, no real progress for the Rights of women can be achieved in Nigeria .

The Protocol to the African Charter on Human Rights

The protocol was adopted on 11 July 2003 by the AU to strengthen the promotion and protection of women's rights. The preamble highlights several considerations necessitating the protocol. These considerations include a recognition of Article 2 of the African Charter on Human and Peoples' Rights, which enshrines the principle of non-discrimination. It includes Article 18, which calls on all states to eliminate discrimination against women. It also includes provisions which recognise women's essential role in development, the principle of promoting gender equality as enshrined in the Consultative Act of the AU as well as the New Partnership for Africa's Development. The considerations also take into account other relevant declarations, resolutions and decisions which underline the commitment of African states to ensure the full participation of African women as equal partners in Africa's development. By virtue of the protocol, Nigerian women are guaranteed the right to dignity; the right to life, integrity and security of persons; freedom from harmful practices which negatively affect the human rights of women; equal rights in marriage; equal rights in

Issues of Concern

cases of separation, divorce and annulment; the right to equal protection and benefit of the law; the right to participate in political and decision making process; the right to a peaceful existence and participation in the promotion and maintenance of peace; the right to education and training; equal opportunity in work and career advancement; the right to health, including sexual and reproductive rights; the right to food security; the right to adequate housing; the right to a positive cultural context; the right to a healthy and sustainable environment; the right to sustainable development; widow's rights; the right to equitable share in inheritance; the right of elderly women to special protection and freedom from violence; the right of women with disabilities to special protection and freedom from violence; the right of women in distress to special protection; and a right of remedy to any woman whose right or freedom has been violated.

The obligation of the Nigerian government under the protocol includes ensuring that women enjoy the rights mentioned above through the following actions:

(a)Enactment of appropriate legislation to combat all forms of discrimination, and specifically to prohibit all forms of violence against women; to ensure prevention, punishment and eradication of violence against women; to prohibit and punish all forms of genital mutilation; to guarantee that no marriage takes place without free will

Issues of Concern

and between consenting adults; to ensure that men and women have the same right during separation, divorce and annulment of marriage; and to guarantee equal opportunity in work and career advancement.

(b) Appropriate and effective education, administration, prohibition, protection, promotion, institutional, implementation and regulatory measures.

(c) Integrating a gender perspective in policy decision.

(d) Modifying social and cultural patterns of conduct of women and men through public education, information and communication.

(e) Positive action to promote participation of women in politics and decision-making.

(f) Provision of effective remedies.

(g) Ensuring full implementation at the national level.

Issues of Concern

(h) Providing budgetary and other resources necessary for full and effective implementation. So far, some of the positive actions taken by the Nigeria government are:

- Adoption of a gender policy in 2007;

- Establishment of science schools for girls;

- Establishment of women development centres in 36 states;

- Adoption of the Trafficking in Person's (Prohibition) Law Enforcement and Administration Act;

- Establishment of a national agency for the prohibition of trafficking in persons;

- Adoption of a national policy on HIV/AIDS, reproductive health and female genital mutilation.

Aspects hindering the rights of women includes:

The patriarchal structure of Nigerian society;

*Failure of the National Assembly to pass the abolition Of all forms Of discrimination against Women In Nigeria And Other Related Matters Bill and failure to pass a national bill prohibiting violence against women.

Issues of Concern

*Failure of the government to domesticate the protocol or enact appropriate legislation necessary for bringing to pass its obligations and undertakings under the protocol is worrying. The questions that come to mind are: Why did the Nigerian government sign the protocol? Did the government sign as a mere formality, knowing that the protocol could be frustrated by non-domestication by virtue of Section 12 of the Constitution? Or is there just a divorce between the arm of government that signs international instrument and the arm that domesticates these agreements? Or do we align our thinking with Richard Falk, who says: 'For various reasons associated with public opinion and prides, governments are quite ready to endorse (even formerly) standards of human rights despite their unwillingness to uphold these standards in practice.'

The Nigerian Reality: Despite the provisions of the protocol recognising and guaranteeing rights and the obligation of the Nigeria government, the lives of Nigerian women is yet to attain a commensurate level of improvement. Women rank lower than men in all indices of development in the country.

Economic and Social Welfare Rights : Paul Ogunyomi, writing on the typologies of discriminative practices in the Nigerian workplace, identified sex discrimination as being prevalent in Nigeria. This takes

Issues of Concern

the form of a woman being treated less favourably than a man on the grounds of sex, or indirectly by conditions applied equally to men and women which are detrimental to women.

Research reveals that adequate maternity leave is important to enable the women's body to recover after delivery. A study of the Nigerian workplace has revealed that '...gap is identified between law and practice with wide patterns of protection resulting in some women enjoying good benefits, while others are wholly or partly unprotected within the Nigeria workplace...'

Women still have a higher unemployment rate than men. Those employed are concentrated in the informal sectors like agriculture, petty trading and services. Home-making is still not recognised or compensated.

Health and Reproductive Rights: With a maternal mortality ratio of 704 to 1,000 per 100,000 live births, Nigeria continues to have one of the highest levels of maternal mortality. Incidences of gender-based violence have health consequences and result in health complications including miscarriages, long term disabilities, unwanted pregnancies, HIV/AIDS and other sexually transmitted diseases.

Issues of Concern

Right to Education and Training: Access to education is still low, especially in the northern parts of the country where withdrawal of girls for the purposes of marriage or for care giving is still practiced. According to Action Aid, '...educational developments in northern Nigeria is lagging behind other parts of the country on practically every indicator, number of facilities, transition rates, girls enrolment, number of teachers...The girls are hawking wares or doing household chores...Low girls enrolment is bound to aggravate gender imbalances that skews present and future opportunities against women.' Nation-wide, gender gaps still exist at the higher levels of education.

Right to Participation in Political and Decision Making Processes: Significant advances have been made in the area of women's participation in governance, yet the political participation of women in Nigeria remains one of the lowest in the world. Women's participation in government is still below the 35 per cent stipulated in the gender policy.

Marriage, Separation, Divorce and Women's Property Rights: Although Article 7 of the protocol provides for both parties of a marriage to enjoy equal rights within and after the marriage, in issues of custody and access to an equitable share of the joint property deriving from the marriage, this is not the case. Three forms of

Issues of Concern

marriages are recognized in Nigeria - customary, Islamic and legislative marriage. The reality of women married under customary and Islamic law has not yet been affected by the protocol. A woman married under customary law is entitled to be provided with a home by her husband as long as the marriage lasts. She is also entitled to use her husband's property, but cannot dispose of it as her own. The right to be provided with a house by her husband terminates upon divorce. Upon divorce, a woman married under customary law has no claim over a house jointly owned by her husband. Her position is not helped by the provisions of the Matrimonial Causes Act in respect of maintenance and settlement of property, which expressly excludes the application of its provisions to marriages under customary and Islamic law. However in the case of women married under law, where she is able to produce documents showing she made a contribution to the property, she is entitled to the part of the property commensurate to her contribution. Many women are denied custody and access to their children. Among those under Islamic law, child marriage is still prevalent. According to BAOBAB for Women's Human Rights, '...girls are often married between the ages of 9-14. The occurrence of child marriage is common.'

Violence Against Women: The protocol guarantees women freedom from violence. In reality, there is a prevalence of violence against women in our society. Violence takes several forms, including domestic violence, early and forced marriages, female genital mutilation, widow torture and inheritance related violence.

Issues of Concern

There are also direct forms of violence against women in Nigeria. For instance, in discussing the impact of the activities of militias, cults and security forces on women in the Niger Delta, Emem Okon states, '...When a culture of armed gang violence takes root in a society that does not recognise and respect women's rights, the result is a higher level of gender-based violence against women. In this case, the proliferation of guns in the Niger Delta has increased the risk that girls and women will be targets of sexual assault.' In another section of the same article, she stated that, 'The consequence has been disastrous, as women have suffered massive massacre, rape, sexual abuse, social psychological trauma...aggravated poverty, unemployment, hunger, anger, low self-esteem, bitterness, frustration, desperation, fear, tension and more conflicts.'

Some violence is performed by law enforcement agents. This can be direct or indirect. Direct assault by security officers is becoming prevalent. For instance, a case was brought before the Gwagwalada High Court in Abuja in which a police man raped two girls. In the Odioma community of Brass Local Government in the Niger Delta, Amnesty International reported a case where a rape victim described

Issues of Concern

how She was raped alongside her mother by security officers. Two-months pregnant at the time, she lost her baby.

Access to Justice and Equal Protection Under the Law: The Constitution and certain laws in Nigeria still contain discriminatory aspects. For instance, Section 26(2) of the Constitution does not allow a Nigerian woman to transmit her nationality to her husband if he is a foreigner. Section 55 of the Penal Code applicable in northern Nigeria permits wife battery as chastisement, as long as grievous harm is not afflicted. Section 55 of the Labour Act prohibits women from working in the night.

Elimination of Harmful Practices, Culture, and Discrimination Against Women: In some parts of Nigeria, women are still regarded as part of the husband's property and as such she cannot inherit her husband's property, but must be inherited alongside his other property by another male of the family. Also 'a lot of customs still continue unabated...that infringe greatly on the human rights of women'.

According to the National Human Rights Commission (NHRC), challenges to the promotion and protection of women's rights still

Issues of Concern

include harmful tradition practices such as female genital mutilation, widowhood rites, child marriage and violence against women.

Right to Inheritance: In most parts of Nigeria, female children are still discriminated against on issues of inheritance. With the decision in Mojekwu v Mojekwu, in which the Court of Appeal declared the 'oli-ekpe' custom of Nnewi - which permits the son or the brother of a deceased person to inherit his property to the exclusion of his female children - discriminatory, it was expected that discrimination against women and the girl child on the issue of inheritance would end. This is definitely not the reality, probably because the decision has not gained nationwide popularity and poverty prevents women from going to court to assert their rights.

Poverty and the Right to Dignity, Food Security and Adequate Housing: One major hindrance to the right to dignity, food security and adequate housing in Nigeria is poverty. Although Nigeria is richly endowed with both human and material resources, the Nigerian government, Nigerian civil society and the UNDP all state that approximately 70 per cent of Nigerians as poor. The majority of the poor are women. Also, Nigeria does not have a social security plan for providing food and housing to the poor. This makes the situation of women precarious and exposes them to the sex trade and destitution.

The Right to A Healthy Environment and Sustainable Development: Every woman in Nigeria has a right to a healthy environment that is favourable to their development. In reality, the environment in Nigeria has not been favourable to the development of women.

According to Abiola and Iyare, 'Since oil struck four decades ago, the ecological and environmental hazards from indiscriminate exploration have constituted an affront on the community and the survival of its people...the effects of oil exploration has produced debilitating effects on the peoples traditional occupation - fishing and farming...'.

When the environment is degraded, as is the current situation in Nigeria, women are most affected because of their culturally and socially defined roles and responsibilities, because their adaptive capacity is low due to poverty and because their livelihoods are tied to the environment. In sum, any damage to the environment is damage to women as it affects their potential and their productivity.

Recommendations

The rich provisions of the protocol recognising and guaranteeing women's human rights in Nigeria promises a beautiful future for women - if the government fulfils its obligations.

In light of the current realities, government should redeem its image and show its commitment by:

- Domesticating the protocol;

- Passing the bill on violence against women;

- Reviewing laws on women's property rights and all other laws discriminating against women;

- Adequate budgetary allocations to issues that promote women's rights and bridge gender gaps;

- Integrating women's right issues and gender education into the school curriculum.

References

Case laws

Akinubi Vs Akinubi

Coker Vs Coker

General electric Company Vs Gilbert

Mojekwu vs mojekwu

Okwueze vs Okwueze

Olowu vs Olowu

Thomasia Ayoola Ricardo vs John Lajorin Abal

Books

1. 1999 constitution of the Federal Republic of Nigeria
2. Constitution of the Federal Republic of Nigeria (First Alteration Act 2010)
3. Constitution of the federal Republic of Nigeria (second Alteration Act 2010)
4. Amnesty international (1995) Human Rights are Women's Right
5. Cock Rebecca J; ed, Human Rights of Women: national and international perspectives

6. Walter Lynn, ed. Women's Rights: A Global view, Westport, Conn; Greenwood press, 2001

Online Research

http://www.wildaf-ao.org

http://hrw.org

http://web.africa.ufl.edu

Acronyms

CEDAW   Convention on the Elimination of all Forms of Discrimination against Women

CSW   Commission on the Status Of Women

IWY   International Women's Year

NGO   Non-governmental Organisation

PC   Penal Code

THE CHARTER The Charter on Human and People's Rights

UDHR   Universal Declaration of Women's Rights

UN   United Nations

VVF   Vesico Vagina Fitula

WILDAF   Women In Law

WIN   Women In Nigeria

Note

Note

Note

Note

3099956R00051

Printed in Great Britain
by Amazon.co.uk, Ltd.,
Marston Gate.